SPOTLIGHT ON POETRY
WHAT KIND OF POEM? 1

Contents

Collected by Brian Moses and David Orme

Collins

Acknowledgements

Whilst every effort has been made to contact the copyright-holders
and to secure the necessary permission to reprint these selections,
this has not proved to be possible in every case. The publishers
would appreciate any information which would allow them to do so.

'Riddle' by Michaela Morgan; 'Squeezes' by Brian Patten, published
by permission of the author. First published in *Gargling with Jelly*
(Puffin Books); 'We Want to Wear Our Wellies' by David Ward;
'There's a Hole in My Pants' by John Foster, © John Foster, 1996.
First published in *You Little Monkey* (OUP). Reproduced by
permission of the author; 'A is For...' by Lucy Coates, © Lucy
Coates. First published in *First Rhymes* by Lucy Coates, Orchard
Books Limited; 'Down in the Hollow' by Michaela Morgan; 'Animal
Riddles' by Marian Swinger; 'Fireworks!' by Judith Nicholls;
'November Night Countdown' by Moira Andrew; 'How To Tell a
Klotz From a Glotz' from *Oh Say Can You Say* © Dr. Seuss
Enterprises, L.P. 1979. All rights reserved. Used by permission.

Published by Collins Educational
An imprint of HarperCollins*Publishers*
77–85 Fulham Palace Road
Hammersmith
London W6 8JB

www.fireandwater.com

© HarperCollins*Publishers* 1999

First published 1999

Reprinted 0 9 8 7 6 5 4 3 2 1

ISBN 0 00 310 342 0

Designed by Clare Truscott
Cover design by Clare Truscott and Kate Roberts
Illustrations by Tim Archbold, Michaela Bloomfield, Louise Drake
Lee, Melanie Mansfield, Andrew Midgley, Ben Morris, Lisa Smith,
Stephen Waterhouse

Printed and bound in Scotland by Scotprint

Collins Educational would like to thank the following teachers and
consultants who contributed to the research of this series:

Maria Artoon (Barnfield School); Mrs J. Bibby (St Paul's C of E
Primary); Jenny Cox (Melcombe Primary School); Jason Darley, Liz
Hooley (Jessop Primary School); Mrs M.G. Farnell (High Meadow
First School); Ann Hughes; Karina Law; Alison Lewis; Louise
Lochner, Gateway Primary School; Chris Lutrario; Lesley Moores
(Princess Royal Primary School); Hannah O'Gorman (St Edward's
Primary School); Sally Prendergrast (Brooke Hill School); Jenny
Ransom; Betty Root; Sheila Stamp and Michael Webster (Castle
Lower School); Shri Toplek, Westminster City School; Jill Walkinton;
Sue Webb; Jill Wells (St Andrews C of E Primary School).

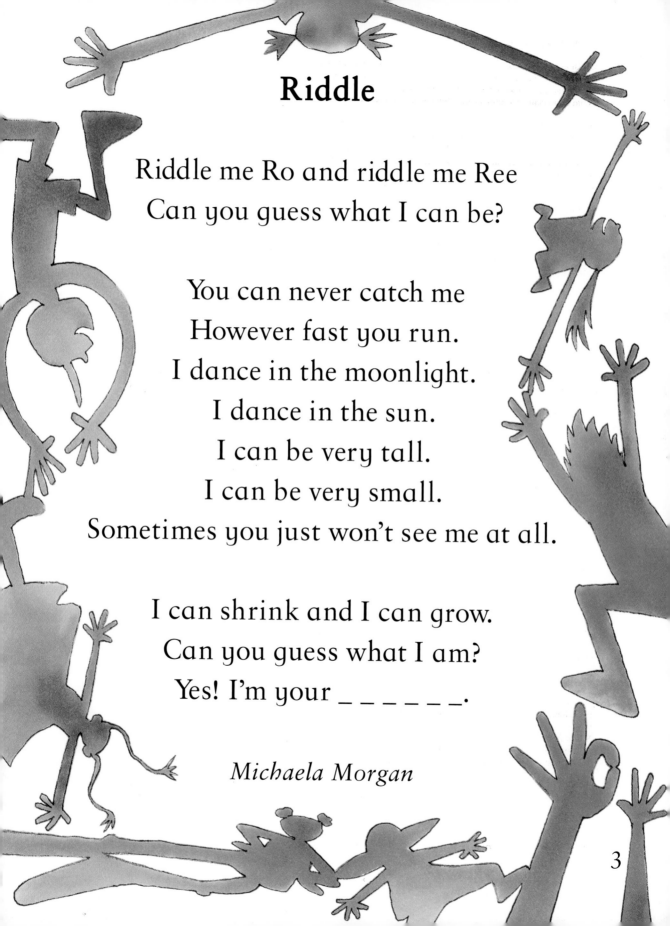

Riddle

Riddle me Ro and riddle me Ree
Can you guess what I can be?

You can never catch me
However fast you run.
I dance in the moonlight.
I dance in the sun.
I can be very tall.
I can be very small.
Sometimes you just won't see me at all.

I can shrink and I can grow.
Can you guess what I am?
Yes! I'm your _ _ _ _ _ _.

Michaela Morgan

Squeezes

We love to squeeze bananas,
We love to squeeze ripe plums,
And when they are feeling sad
We love to squeeze our mums.

Brian Patten

We Want to Wear Our Wellies

We want to wear our wellies
When it's windy.
We want to wear our wellies
When it's wet.
We want to wear our wellies
When the Weather on the telly
Says it's going to be
The warmest day yet.

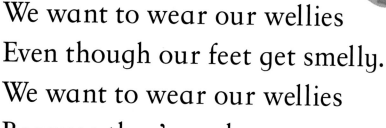

We want to wear our wellies
Even though our feet get smelly.
We want to wear our wellies
Because they're red.
We want to wear out wellies
When it's wet or warm or windy –
But we never wear our wellies in bed!

Dave Ward

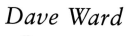

There's a Hole in My Pants

There's a hole in my pants.
It's our washing machine.
It's eating our clothes,
Not washing them clean.

As it churns round and round,
It snorts and it snickers,
Chewing holes in Dad's shirts
And ripping Mum's knickers.

It's swallowed a sock.
We can't open the door.
It's bubbling out soap suds
All over the floor.

There's a monster that lives
In our washing machine.
It's eating our clothes,
Not washing them clean.

John Foster

Topsy-Turvy Land

The people walk upon their heads,
The sea is made of sand,
The children go to school by night,
In Topsy-Turvy Land.

The front-door step is at the back,
You're walking when you stand,
You wear your hat upon your feet,
In Topsy-Turvy Land.

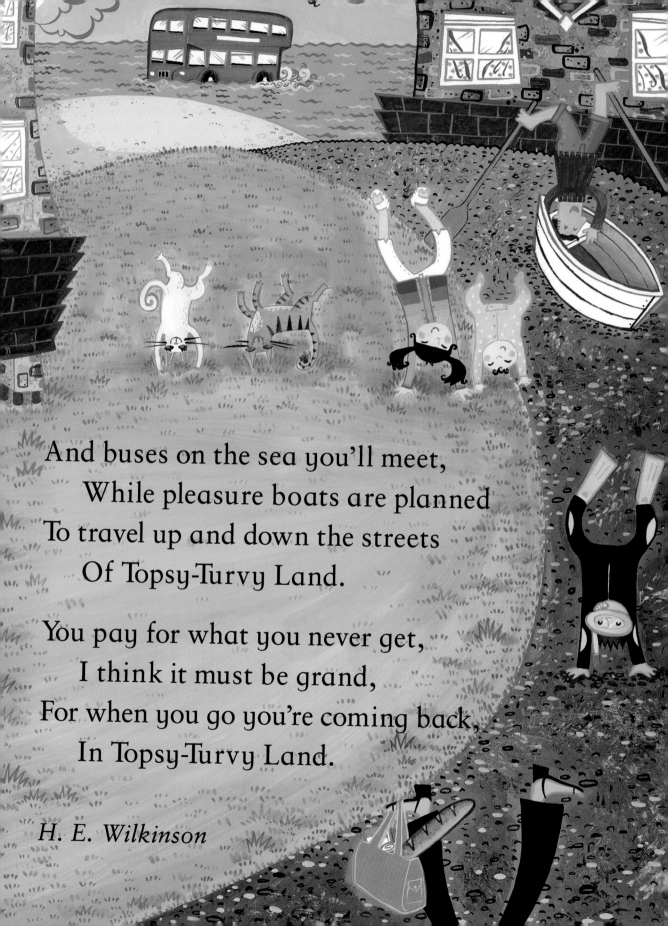

And buses on the sea you'll meet,
  While pleasure boats are planned
To travel up and down the streets
  Of Topsy-Turvy Land.

You pay for what you never get,
  I think it must be grand,
For when you go you're coming back,
  In Topsy-Turvy Land.

H. E. Wilkinson

A is For...

A is for aeroplane

B is for bird

C is for clouds in the sky.

D is for duckling

E is for egg

F is for feather and fly.

G is for Granny
H is for hugs
I is for "I love you too!".

J is for jellyfish
K is koala
L is for lions in the zoo.

M is for marmalade
N is for nuts
O is for olives with stones.

P is for palace
Q is for queen
R is for royal red thrones.

S is for storms
T is for tempest
U is "Umbrellas up, please!".

V is for violin
W is whistle
X is for xylophone keys.

Y is for yellow and yoghurt and yacht
and yawns when you've had a late night
Z is for zebra and zigzag and zoom
and zipping your jacket up tight.

Lucy Coats

Down in the Hollow

Down in the hollow where the trees grow low
    a cat's on the prowl, creeping slow.
She's prowling, she's growling soft and low
    growl, growl, growl (soft and low).

Down in the hollow where the trees grow low,
    an owl's on the prowl, swooping low.
Swooping and whooping, soft and low,
    Too whit, too whooo (soft and low).

Down in the hollow where the trees grow low,
a dog's on the prowl, creeping slow.
Prowling and growling then BOW WOW WOW
He sees the cat and what do you know!

"Bow wow!" says the dog "I've got you now!"
"Too whit" says the owl "How? How? How?"
"Miaow" says the cat "Can't catch me now
I'm climbing UP this tree and I won't come down!"

Michaela Morgan

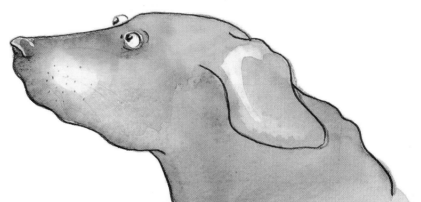

Animal Riddles

It has four hooves, a tail of course.
Who wants to ride this lovely...

It's dressed in feathers, rhymes with carrot
sharp curved beak, must be a...

It's long, and skinny as a rake.
Don't let it bite, must be a...

It's small and scuttles round the house.
A long, thin tail, must be a...

Long ears, bright eyes, a hopping habit,
round white tail, must be a...

You count them when you're trying to sleep.
Those woolly jumpers, must be...

Marian Swinger

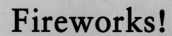

Fireworks!
(A chant for two groups of voices)

Squibs and sparklers
Squibs and sparklers
Golden showers
Golden showers
Shooting stars and Catherine wheels
Shooting stars and Catherine wheels
Fiery flowers
Fiery flowers
Racing rockets
Racing rockets
Whirling windmills
Whirling windmills
Flashing fountains
Flashing fountains
Blazing mountains
Blazing mountains

Light the paper...
Watch them whizzing
Watch them whizzing
Watch them whizzing
B A N G !

Judith Nicholls

19

November Night Countdown

Ten fat sausages
    sizzling in the fire.
Nine fiery flames
    reaching ever higher.

Eight jumping jacks
    leaping on the ground.
Seven silver sparklers
    whirling round and round.

Six golden fountains
    fizzing in the dark.
Five red rockets
    whizzing across the park.

Four bright Catherine wheels
spinning on the gate.
Three wide-eyed children
allowed out very late.

Two proud parents
watching all the games.
One lonely Guy
roasting in the flames.

Moira Andrew

How To Tell a Klotz From a Glotz

Well, the Glotz, you will notice,
has lots of black spots.
The Klotz is quite different
with lots of black dots.
But the big problem is
that the spots on a Glotz
are about the same size
as the dots on a Klotz.
So you first have to spot
who the one with the dots is.
Then it's easy to tell
who the Klotz or the Glotz is.

Dr Seuss

Glossary

A is for...

koala small bear-like animal from Australia

thrones special chairs for kings and queens

tempest powerful storm

xylophone musical instrument with wooden bars that are hit to make sounds

Animal Riddles

scuttles runs quickly with very small steps

Fireworks!

squibs fireworks that go BANG!

November Night Countdown

jumping jacks fireworks that jump and go BANG!

Catherine wheels spinning fireworks

Guy the stuffed figure of a man (Guy Fawkes) that is burnt on bonfires

Index of poems by title

Index of poems by first line